We Face the Tremendous Meat on the Teppan

NAOKO FUJIMOTO

POETRY

C&R Press
Conscious & Responsible

All Rights Reserved

Printed in the United States of America

First Edition
2 3 4 5 6 7 8 9

Selections of up to two pages may be reproduced without permission. To reproduce more than two pages of any one portion of this book write to C&R Press publishers John Gosslee and Andrew Sullivan.

Cover art by Tana Oshima

Copyright ©2022 Naoko Fujimoto

ISBN 978-1-949540-35-2

C&R Press
Conscious & Responsible
crpress.org

For special discounted bulk purchases, please contact:
C&R Press sales@crpress.org
Contact info@crpress.org to book events, readings and author signings.

We Face the Tremendous Meat on the Teppan

We Face the Tremendous Meat on the Teppan (2- 27)

Section i	2
iii	3
iv	4
v	5
vii	6
ix	8
xi	9
xiii	12
xiv	14
xv	15
xvii	17
xix	18
xxii	20
xxiii	22
xxiv	23
xxv	25
xxvii	26
xxviii	27

We Face the Tremendous Meat on the Teppan

i.

*Amazon Alexa,
remind me, hard—*

ii.

Nagoya Castle is not a real castle—,
        made of concrete with two large elevators
        and laminated stairs, slippery during rainy season,
        splashes making my shoes squeak

    and I slip, hit my forehead
        Firecrackers scatter inside aluminum pots.

*

        Now, I hear
        Fusuma, fusuma! People scream.

                              Oh, I am time-traveling.

I stand in the burning chaos
        holding a fusuma (a large sliding paper door)

     and a few miles away,

              Grandmother slides into a ditch
              where a horse hides
              (this is why I will be born after forty years), though
              Nagoya Castle is
                          not extinguished.

People are running like blind beetles
                          in rains of—
                          rains of bullets.
                          Dust plugs her ears and nose—

her head crouches down a hole by the ditch over a small bridge,
and then in slow-motion when the bridge collapses—

a tail brushes her face.
        "Oh my, I am with an *Omma-sama*."

iii.

The *Kinshachi* on the castle
    (is a golden nugget; perhaps, large, shrimp tempura-like)
    is tilted at first, then starts melting,

        extremely hot eighteen-karat gold,
        slowly sinking into the ceramic roof—
        swallowed up by this war hole.

        *

        I am watching a super nova—
        sparks of copper, iron nails,
        vaporizing gold,

        burning cypress pillar
                            ash winged ants.

        It is horrifyingly   beautiful.

iv.

Fusuma, fusuma!
A man hands me another paper door;

from the tatami room
where the Tokugawa Shogunate slept twice
after passing rooms and rooms of fusuma paintings.

People dump water onto their heads,
(men and women both, they rush back and forth)
grab more fusuma. And more paintings—

>panels of hills by the seashore,
>boats float in
>
>whispers of silver-grass;
>unreachable silk holograms
>illuminate human hearts.
>
>Two thousand years ago,
>a sleepless Japanese poet sang
>
>a song of a carbonated moon
>on a decaying boat with tangled
>dragnets
>separating his wife and two
>daughters.
>
>A pale white, Japanese tit
>pecks its predator's brain. Peck
>and peck,   peck,
>peck, peck flint sparks,

one fusuma starts flaring—
the tit, or sparrow,
or some kind of bird still sits on a branch
(maybe a peach tree?)
like burnt toast, quietly turning brown—

v.

>*Amazon Alexa, take pictures*, I scream

but there is no phone (of course),
my fingers are scorched.

>It is May 14, 1945,

the bombing of Nagoya in World War II
by the North American B-25 Mitchell
nearly four thousand people died that day.

vi.

                                        That is why.

                                                *

That is why

there are several blank,
fusuma in their restored rooms in the castle.

The historian cannot bring back burnt papers.

vii.

    Grandmother
    melts
    away backwards,
    crawling into her nest
    on the branch
    that shakes every minute.

    Cogwheels spiral
    downward,
    deeper and further
    until her steps
    do not appear
    in the desert of time.

    A woodpecker nips
    worms under the bark
        the bird nibbles
            memories of why she is wandering around—

        she is here, so I am here
        (the simplest equation)

viii.

but how long does she keep eating the tremendous meat for us—
at the same restaurant (rebuilt) where Mr. Suzuki took
Grandfather in 1938.

Mr. Suzuki came back from Java—
the island colonized by the Dutch, and then the Japanese—
He had never put on geta-slippers
like the Japanese men around these streets;

instead, he wore the softest hemp suits,
a beautifully pressed hat, and black enamel shoes with socks.

He took Grandfather
to a French restaurant that day before the war.

The menu, written in cursive, lay next to
marmalade in a tiny porcelain cup. He taught
Grandfather how to put butter on a baguette.

Together they learned foreign languages in college
from an old Japanese professor—
they were innocent back then, ignorant of
the flavors contained in these little colorful jam jars.

                        Next year, Mr. Suzuki received
a bright red note, recruited to the Philippines
and trampled by unknown insects until his last breath.

ix.

        Grandfather's boots were sopping wet;
        rain and bullets pummeled a mud hedge.
        His fellow Japanese dragged their paralyzed legs.

Their hands did not smell human.
        Dead bodies smoldered from toes to fingers.

        His commander rolled them over with a long pole.

Their eyes stare empty.

Need more dry wood to cover their bodies.

x.

Can I save Grandfather's best friend?

Can I remove a starter of B-25 just like nuns did in the Sound of Music?

Can I keep peach, I mean, peace?

xi.

I was five. I wet my underwear

sitting for a long time on the wooden floor
where my teacher reads a story about a rabbit
folding its clothes beside a pool
(our swimming lesson starts the next day).

Warmth leaked out
from under my skirt, naked bottomed;

I hid it in my blazer jacket.　　　　　Later I told Grandmother
how genius it was not to wear the underwear,
and tried to show it to her;

but I could not find it in my right pocket.
It appeared in the left pocket
of someone else's blazer.
(Fact is, we collected feathers that day too.)

Remember,
right is for your Chapstick hand
you silly, Grandmother said.

xii.

    In her kitchen, an empty kettle
    boils over the gas ring.
       A bag of tea sugar spills. Into the dark

narrow pit
boring through
everything in front of them,
ants forget

their fellow's name who broke its legs
seventeen feet after the wooden floor,
or got washed away by the drainage leak.
Grandmother crushes one between her fingers and says, *Ant,*

      who are you my darling?

        From our cracked screen door
        through drywall,

                    and resting on a decayed beam
                    under the kitchen,

              under the toaster oven—
              crawling over bread crumbs,

        or clinging to strawberry jam on the counter.
        Even though I spray

    after every meal,
    they find the drop of

crystalized mirin-sake,
a grain of fried rice. I hate their skills.

xiii.

The annoying ants
gather around a licked lollipop

hands and legs stuck in
melting sugar resin

slowly covering the pores
on their shoulders, suffocating them.

I see those black balls
(cannot tell what the flavors are)
on the parking lot,

some are on chewing gum
(watermelon, perhaps)

sucking sweet particles
into their stomachs

later they will share it (if they survive)
with their queen and young.

Only the crusty old (but macho)
are allowed to go outside of their nests,

their young stay under the soil
deep and wide,

I cannot reach their colony;
though, they move a lot

for a better habitation
making their new entrance and path.

I fascinatingly
hate their skills

and want to sink my house into the River Nile,
ants will drown

(we float in plastic doughnuts to see this)
but no—

grabbing hand and foot, ants make a sphere
and move forward like a cogwheel

swimming and breathing as they turn and turn,
rolling to the shore.

They live in Egypt on the Earth, and might be on Mars too
profound, near the core of the planet.

Humans are so lackadaisical—
too busy painting ceramic bowls,

adding spikes on to their edges,
putting them on the bookshelf.

Do we forget why we survive?
Are vermin wiser than humans?

xiv.

To the queen,
(shall I call her a dictator?)
they carry flecks to feed their descendants.

If they lose the queen,
they will be slaves outside their territory
or they die off with the queen.

What is new to us
making our mortal bodies,

amino acids and vitamins,
five-hour energy drinks
anti-aging creams,

gummy bears for our children
who never shut up.

I ask again,
what is new to us,

after we trade the ceramic bowls,
cut peaches from our neighbors' trees.

xv.

Do we forget why we survive?
            bless us for tomorrow's war.
We will dump a hell of a lot of bombs onto the city (cities).
Pins on the map.
One lightly rolls
            down the table to the floor.

xvi.

I squeeze my head
like a moray eel

through the narrow entrance
down an extremely long staircase
screaming *your* name toward *your* world.

            terrified to end up in the place
            Grandmother is (was) in.

I remember Grandmother's sobbing.
She wants a divorce;
instead she scrubs bathtubs for sixty-seven years.

An abandoned refrigerator—
fried oysters caked in salt,
sake, and rotten cabbage. Unpaid bills.

She lights the kitchen stove

and kerosene-oil heaters.
Azuki-beans drain in the strainer.

No sugar yet. Bitterness must be gone,
Grandmother says.

I change the water
and place them back in the pot
again and again.

All the windows fog.
Cooking air condenses.
                       Can I add sugar now, Obāchan?

She curls her back and falls asleep.
Her forehead touches the tatami-mattress.

xvii.

        I find teacups out
        at 2:30 in the morning, and
        her crouching by the entrance,
        looking for her invisible brothers' shoes

her red lipstick
on a half-closed mouth
showing jagged teeth.

xviii.

Dear God,
Dear Omma-sama,
Dear Someone Who'll Listen to me.

Is age full of promises

after cracking a heart open like a peanut shell,

pieces drop on the steps for
birds that will never dot the path?

xix.

Grandmother will die eventually;
maybe six months from now,
(in three years, she will be a hundred years old)

but we still offer her
a brand new pacemaker
a knee replacement
                              Obāchan, we need your smile.

I will probably not see
her last breath and hold her ice-cold,

soft hands

that worked through her entire life.
Her blank eyes stare at something that is no longer there, her feet
rough from the spilled sugar.

                                    xx.

                              It is what it is, isn't it?
                              It *is* what it is.
                              It is what it *is*.
                              Shōganai

                              Is it really *Shōganai*?

That word is hard to translate into English,

unlike sakura,
komorebi,
tsunami,

The direct translation of
Shōganai
is
the mole around Grandmother's waist
(rapidly growing),
one hair sticking out of

its center of dark brown melanin (that is why she thinks
        her beauty is incomplete), *Obāchan*,
                      it is
                      Shōganai, isn't it?

xxi.

The first time I painted
liquid foundation on my face
it made a luminous glow—,
a very fair palette.
My face floated on my neck,
peeling like an old portrait.	I panicked
in a public restroom and cried—
cried with Mother by Grandmother's hospital bed.

Her wish was to have me
shed like a holy snake.
After puffing snow powder on my face,
she pinched my cheek bones. *There is a beautiful girl.*

*

NO!
Your skin is still Kuroi (black)!

xxii.

        Grandmother grinned

        when we celebrated her hundredth birthday
        at the restaurant with
        a view of the concrete castle.

Both my parents,
both grandparents (still alive),
my great-grandmother (partially alive),

we all watch steak grilling
medium-rare on the teppanyaki

watermelons
extra-sweet green tea.

We worship in the graveyard
where our ancestors
and two dogs are buried.

Mother used to say,
it's against Buddhism, remove the animal

before she met my cat,
curling its tail around our legs.

My great-great grandmother says,
you do not get pregnant because the cat sucks out your love

and they all moan that there is no descendant to light incense—
                                                        burnt bones
occupy the plates,   we are mouthfuls of meat.

So,
during the war,
raw fluid flowed between my thighs,

        is this appropriate conversation
        while having raspberry sherbet, *Obāchan?*

After all,
I have plenty of maxi pads
every twenty-eight days for the last twenty-three years,
for which I am thankful,

I tell Grandmother sixty-seven times during the meal.

xxiii.

                                              And I
plug an outlet to turn on a vacuum cleaner
after I force Grandmother to sit down in a chair
brushing sugar off the bottom of her socks

                        or artificial sweetener
                        that spilled
                        all over her dining room floor.

A jet crosses over us,
        the engine's sound piercing,
        but it's not a combat plane
        the plane carries a passenger
        like my husband, American.
                I am here

                I am sitting next to you, *Obāchan,*
                Don't shake, do not shake   *any more.*

xxiv.

Why does she trap herself
in the last weeks of World War II?

she recites a Buddhist sutra
is worried about her two older brothers
whom I have never met,

cannot even point them out
in a black and white photo album.
The vacation pictures may have burned
when they ran from the fire.

        The two brothers' hands
        smell not human
        with so much dry wood in the ditches.

        How hard to smolder bodies
        from toes to fingers;
        drops on the gravel.

        *

A squall batters the roof.
She conceals her body from raining bullets,
hot and humid, no streaks of light.

Sweat rolls between my hairs as I
listen to cicadas and her imaginary horse;
her eyes grim,
gazing at me.

Does not matter how her heart keeps pumping
right now,
I want to know when her appropriate time is.
Will she have more time to mourn than the others?

Can her two dead brothers (and I) lift her
to the place
where lotus flowers are in full glory;

with no pumpkins, potatoes, or daikon-radishes, please,
Grandmother said.

She flipped the vegetables back to a plastic bag;
especially pumpkin seeds (they remind her of starvation)

and with her parchment fingers,
she added a lump of sugar
into my palm
it tasted bitter like nails
turned to dust
sunlight baked every part of her body

in this smallest island
unexploded shells still rest under the soil.
Take them home, will you?

xxv.

On that day,
her mother waited long enough to believe
                              her dead
so she bathed her child until the skin became bright pink
and cooked beautiful white rice to celebrate
(*it was an inappropriate thing to do*, Grandmother said, again)
and weak miso soup with plants from their vine field.

        Can you believe my mother had never seen
        pumpkins until she was 20 years old?

In her cooking class, she said,

"What is this?"

xxvi.

                Let me run.

I jumped off the highest jungle gym in elementary school.
Osteoporosis is not on my checklist

(my female ancestors never had it).

They did not hold me when I was a child, though.
Taxidermic birds
nodded their heads
counting my breaths in and out.

xxvii.

If I breathe in and out,
the candle flame and trembles.
Not enough candles
on a birthday cake, and

one extra candle for the Buddhist altar
(the great uncles partially inside. Their bodies were not found during the war.)

Have I seen a burning field?

Like spring in Nara, how beautiful
it is to smell flaming hills;
the nostrils darkly irritated
deep inside.

Grandmother
does not like the burning
and her tongue spits out
this twenty-seconds birthday song.

xxviii.

In the late evening,
she says, I was born under the luckiest planet;
after she washes her face,

a meteor shower falls from the sky.
        Some shells rattle;
                some crash
                        adding rubble,

more rubble to rebuild and destroy, repeat,
but I do not hang a cloth
around the lamp.

It is   bright.

C&R PRESS CHAPBOOKS

C&R Press hosts two chapbook selection periods from June to September and November to March each year. The Winter Soup Bowl and Summer Tide Pool Chapbook Series are open to new and established writers in poetry, fiction, essay and other creative writing.

2020 Winter Soup Bowl
My Roberto Clemente by Rick Hilles

2019 Summer Tide Pool
Inside the Orb of an Oracle by Dannie Ruth

2019 Winter Soup Bowl
The Magical Negro Reveals His Secret by Gabriel Green

2018 Summer Tide Pool
Yell by Sarah Sousa

2018 Winter Soup Bowl
Paleotemptestology by Bertha Crombet
White Boys from Hell by Jeffrey Skinner

2017 Summer Tide Pool
Atypical Cells of Undetermined Significance by Brenna Womer

2017 Winter Soup Bowl
Heredity and Other Inventions by Sharona Muir
On Inaccuracy by Joe Manning

2016 Summer Tide Pool
Cuntstruck by Kate Northrop
Relief Map by Erin M. Bertram
Love Undefined by Jonathan Katz

2016 Winter Soup Bowl
Notes from the Negro Side of the Moon by Earl Braggs
A Hunger Called Music: A Verse History in Black Music by Meredith Nnoka

www.ingramcontent.com/pod-product-compliance
Lightning Source LLC
Chambersburg PA
CBHW051705040426
42446CB00009B/1313